APRIL MORNING

April Morning

ACE TIWARI

Dedication

To my family and close friends, I am ever so grateful for you all. Thank you for allowing me to express myself freely, laughing boisterously with me instead of at me, and supporting my endeavours that all point towards my ultimate dreams. To me, this poetry collection represents hope, and you all have given that to me.

Copyright © 2025 by Ace Tiwari
All rights reserved. No part of this book may be reproduced in any manner whatsoever without written permission except in the case of brief quotations embodied in critical articles and reviews.
First Printing, 2025

CONTENTS

Dedication - iii

~1~

you and i
1

~2~

the ghost of you
3

~3~

anything
5

~4~

carousel (round and round)
7

~5~

april morning
9

VI ~

~6~

crushed
12

~7~

the rain drowns my heart
14

~8~

how
16

~9~

the lake
18

~10~

i plead (please)
20

~11~

leap (of faith)
22

~12~

met you on a night when the stars didn't glisten
24

~13~

it's haunting me
26

~ VII

~14~

formidable feelings

28

~15~

stay back

30

~16~

never ending walk

32

~17~

stoic boy

34

~18~

shielded

36

~19~

is it?

38

~20~

three weeks later

40

~21~

people pleaser

42

VIII ~

~22~

proceed with caution
45

~23~

sunday afternoon
46

~24~

foreverland
49

~25~

summer nights leave me bleeding
52

~26~

you confuse me to no end
54

~27~

riverflies
57

~28~

there is a path
59

~29~

i am spent
61

~ IX

~30~

jester

63

~31~

beautiful boy (you're lovely)

65

~32~

my favourite otherworldly being

68

~33~

in between here and there

70

~34~

i hope i meet you again.

72

~35~

dear reader

73

~36~

listen

75

~37~

ACKNOWLEDGEMENTS

77

About the Author - 79

~ 1 ~

YOU AND I

when the audience is long gone,
the cleaners are en route home,
and the last light diminishes its glow,
i'll be here, so you're never alone

with thoughts that tarnish your beautiful mind
i will fend off every last worry until
the only thing you're left to worry about is how to breathe
from laughing so hard-

-en your heart, they say.
don't let the tabloids get their way
don't fall for strangers who are simply nice to you
don't forget who you are, i whisper into your hair

and makeup they force onto you to hide who you are.
it is no longer about enunciating your beauty, rather altering it so you can fit into a different mould.
they want the others to like you,
but don't you see that this love is more than enough?

enough, this is getting out of hand.
listen to me: i can love you enough to fill the void of the people who you thought loved you
can't you realise that our love is what makes this life worth living?

the lives we lead that are so different from their own
the queen and the commoner.

when we grow grey hair and lose our teeth,
when they love you no more,
i'll be the last one clapping that standing ovation.
i was the first to tell you of your brains and beauty, and no matter what happens
i promise to be the last.

for you are the blood that runs through my heart, my body, my soul
i do not want to grow old if it's not with you.

with you, i leap from mountain to mountain,
scaling rivers and canyon walls.
with you, i see the sunrise that makes my face glow
with you, i turn the page of my most trying chapter

with you, i am complete.

~ 2 ~

THE GHOST OF YOU

running through moors with sand that spell out your name
racing through forests with rain that wash me clean with the thought of you
recklessly swimming in high tides because life had no meaning until you

i'll chase the ghost of you
wanting to know you like no other
but gone you have,
and alone i fear i am.

you are the curse that has fallen upon me
is this the price i pay for previously not caring?
are you the cure to the disease i have fallen victim to?
lovesickness, homesickness, now i am motion sick

sickly is the complexion i reflect
possessed by the ghost of you
haunting is my voice as i leave consciousness,
leaving home, leaving hell

i call out to the spirits of those who used to love me,
silence returns after a brief hiatus
i cry out to the ghouls of those i loved,
and they regard me with disdain

pushing at all the bruises they gave me,
i decide i've had enough
i think it's time to repay the pain.

~ 3 ~

ANYTHING

you look at me with imploring eyes
wishing that i would open up and
pour my soul to you

i look away
antsy
because i can't explain myself to anyone
not least to you

i don't want to talk about anything
so instead shall we sit in silence?
brooding over what's left unsaid
my favourite thing to do

when i'm with you
i feel like i'm not invisible anymore
i feel like i am a hindrance to your existence
but maybe that's just me and my mind

after i had that unexpected panic attack

you've been more desperate for me to talk than ever
i always thought that you wanted me to shut up
i don't know when to release my hands from the securely fastened zip ties that appeared with my apparel when i was let on this planet

please let's not talk about anything
or think about anything
instead let's watch the sunset and relish in the rain
instead let's kiss until our lips go numb and purple and we don't know what air is anymore

don't look at me with those desperate eyes
i'd rather you tug at my hair aggressively
than gently braid it
please

~ 4 ~

CAROUSEL (ROUND AND ROUND)

round and round we go
circling the border of that vicious cycle that we always seem to near, but never actually cross.
i text you because you get mad at me if i don't,
but you get upset with me, regardless of what i do or don't do.

i called you today
out of the blue to ask "how are you"
you ask what i've been up to
and i tell the truth

big mistake
to trust the two-faced monster
that will rip your skin and shred your bones

why do i keep trusting you?
i know why i oughtn't
and yet
with each bullet you fire at me

i get up and offer the gift once more
shaking in my hands

vulnerability
you dismiss
pushing it out of my hands
and onto the dirt-caked floor

around and around we go
i get so dizzy and my head is spinning
spiralling out of order
so i forget to not trust you
but throughout all this i remain to love you.

~ 5 ~

APRIL MORNING

it's an april morning

   the sun glistens on the serene lake,
   the birds chirp to each other through the leaves of old trees,
   a soft gust of wind passes through the park, upturning a stray paper cup,
   and ruffling your hair ever so slightly

   your glasses catch the glare of golden rays,
   and i am blinded by your beauty

   the sounds of laughing children and a groundskeeper mowing in the distance
   fades away, when you laugh
   i am transfixed by your joy
   and i no longer see or hear anything else

focused

on
  you

  entirely
 utterly
  completely
    aware of you

we meander around the beautiful lake that graces me with your reflection
and we pass a wind chime clinging happily to a tree branch

as we walk back to our discarded picnic, you talk
and i listen to your voice
soft and sweet and melodic
like the very wind chime that sounds in the distance.

comfortable silence falls, and we sit together,
content on my mother's picnic mat that she let me bring today
we look out to the park full of people,
and you make a joke

a reference to a niche subculture that only you introduced me to,
i laugh, proud i understood
your smile widened

and my breath got caught in my throat

i notice the clouds above our heads so
we lie down on the mat, looking up to the sky
i tell you i see a heart, a hat, a horse, a rabbit
you tell me you see a dragon, a leprechaun, a bee, a flower

we giggle at the absurdity of it all
and i can't help but think about
how wondrous it is
to hang out with you.

~ 6 ~

CRUSHED

    an overwhelming, all consuming
crush.

    somehow that word seems insignificant, redundant
    i am being crushed, completely suffocated, lost of air, from the sight of you.
    i am crushed by the diminishing realisation that you won't ever look at me a second time.

    the word "infatuation" is better but doesn't seem entirely accurate either.
    spellbound i am, by your mere existence.
    i see the world through the lens of rose coloured glasses.

    and suddenly all my creativity is being poured into the ways i try to make you notice me, catch the way i look at you, see how funny or intelligent or empathetic i can be.
    i read my poetry aloud and wonder if you know my words are about you,
    directed towards you.

a large part of me hopes you don't, for the mortification following no reciprocation would be a feeling i very well could not bear.
however...
on the off-chance you would give me an opportunity to prove myself,
my heart soars with hope, with possibility
twirling around in the rain, hopping through day to day with a smile on my face,
so high up in the clouds
until rejection brings me crashing down,
crushed.

i read my poems aloud,
scattering my words out into the world,
and i hope you know they're for you.

an insurmountable amount of love i feel,
an abundance of poetry to give.

~ 7 ~

THE RAIN DROWNS MY HEART

you watch the rain as it decorates your bedroom window.
peering out my car window, i watch as one raindrop beats another in the race to reach the end.

shivering, i wrap the family blanket tightly around me.
you light your fireplace, rubbing your hands together and wearing warm fuzzy socks.

(the rain gets heavier)
i go for a walk, holding the umbrella as an accessory, rather than a necessity.
reaching a house i've only ever seen in dreams,
i look up and see a window that is illuminated with colourful lights.

(the rain gets heavier)
the grey skies bore you so on the coloured lights go
playing fiona apple and big thief
you paint and draw and create art that marvels even the greatest
i bask in the brilliance of you

you exit the house you reside in
 walking on
  to the creek you so often escape to

i follow unknowingly
i am just going where the rainbow takes me.
it's windy so the umbrella ditches me,
flying away to join the more exciting
i stand there like a ghost in the middle of the road,
rain trickling past my clothes, into my skin
wet hair hanging around my blemished face.

will i ever see you again?
your porcelain skin, your perfect hair
your striking eyes and the way you stare
right through me like i'm not even there

~ 8 ~

HOW

    will i survive in the world when already i am so taken by you
      so consumed by the thought of you
      so distracted by your existence
      so in love with
    the way you have an immediate response that is so clever and witty and i marvel at your beautiful mind
      no matter how many hues of however many colours it may hold
      i want to know every story you've ever told,
        every friend you've ever made, every pet you've ever had, every person you might've loved.
      i want to be the one you run to when you've got many places to go
      i want to be the one that first hears every update, every event,
        every *thing* you've ever come across
      i want to go through life skipping through fields of wildflowers with you
      i want to know you better than the books you read, the music you listen to
      i want to be the inspiration for the art you create

i would commit a thousand crimes if it meant being with you
   even if our simple existence may already be one.

~ 9 ~

THE LAKE

    wondering if i should venture forward or turn back to the safety of ignorance, i stand
    teetering at the edge of a lake.
    do i dip my toes in the muddy water and relish in the unknown? do i run back to clear skies and dry grass where everything is certain?
    don't i crave change?

    a breeze rustles the leaves at my feet
    a gentle ripple goes across the lake
    and i have never been more tempted

    if i submerge myself under the water, i don't know what will happen
    i don't know what the future holds
    equal chances of the best and the worst await.

    i hear the cries of my fear
    beckoning me back to days of nothing
    i keep my face forward

APRIL MORNING

i want something different,
something *more*

but will i ever move from the edge of the lake?

~ 10 ~

I PLEAD (PLEASE)

please

that word turns sour in my mouth
i gag at the nasty residue it leaves
why should i have to plead for what made me

who i am today
who am i today

will you just let me know
before i go and enter the labyrinth of
what they call my mind

but it is theirs
always has been
never once have i owned it
i've only ever been the victim

of their lies
their twisted truths
their burning slaps

their swinging axe

don't

the contraction of do not
i feel it is overused
"don't do this" "don't do that"
it feels like a smack in the face for a reason i cannot place

but you will, won't you?
just like them
of course
why else was i drawn to you

controlling
aggressive
you have made
a mess of me

but i am not broken
because you can't break something that was never fixed
this makes me grateful
that i was kicked into the dirt so many times

bloody
bruised

i hear their laughs echoing in the distance
no longer do i have the energy to continue this
and so here it ends
as do i

~ 11 ~

LEAP (OF FAITH)

jumping through hoops
and leaping over obstacles i
travelled this far just to catch your eyes
but nothing i do ever seems right

sometimes i wish i inherited the superpower of being able
to properly express my feelings
to the right people instead of trusting the wrong people that will sell
your secrets for the price of popularity

swimming through swamps and
running over rivers i
almost drowned in the pursuit of your heart,
emerald green, precious, glowing,
"made of stone" they say
i think it's easy enough to penetrate

hair i dye, skin i pierce
clothes i change but my accent still remains
will this be enough for you?

will i ever be enough for you

to love
to hold
to take my heart and treat it like your own

canyons i've scaled,
cliff-sides i've climbed,
broke my own heart trying to look into your eyes
to see only darkness reflected in mine.

~ 12 ~

MET YOU ON A NIGHT WHEN THE STARS DIDN'T GLISTEN

clouds covering the stark night sky
and still, i looked up to find the moon
gazing fondly as though i saw it

saddened i was
disheartened by the monday i had just faced
discouraged by the overturned sky
distressed by the amount of academics i had to study

i went outside
looking for a distraction
a wandering cloud, a stray cat
a small ant scurrying along the pavement
and instead
i saw *you*

your hair first caught my eye,
as it was dyed my favourite hue
your eyes took me by surprise,
 so vivid and bright

i was listening to a specific song
playing it over and over and over again
i tried to look away from you
but my eyes latched on like a leech

seeping the colour out of your skin until you were no more
merely a blank canvas i could paint over and make my own

draining the light out of your eyes
until you became someone i could talk to
in my mind, a possessed apparition
puppets guided by the strings of longing

in truth, i don't want to actually be with you
friendship i am complacent with
i just want returned affection
i just want a semblance of your love
even if it may be platonic

god, i need a tonic
to cure me of this curse
a remedy i search for
instead every road i take
leads me back to you.

~ 13 ~

IT'S HAUNTING ME

the sensitivity that i was born with
raised to believe it was inconvenient
annoying, useless
a waste of my tears, a waste of their time

and now it is back
bigger and better than before
now in the form of pleasing others
pleading with the gods

"stop being so sensitive"
turned into
"stop being such a people pleaser"
gets under my skin way too easily

it's like they know how to rile me up
get me defensive then blow down my defences
leaving me vulnerable and defenceless
it's like i'm a defect

i feel like i'm five years old again

are the blotches appearing on your skin caused by the fire i emit?

   don't come too close
     i may burn everything in my vicinity to ashes
   don't come too close
     i may implode and crumple into a pile of ashes
   don't come too close
     you may be able to see the poem in my eyes that reveals my disguise
   don't come too close
     you may realise what i've been trying to hide for so long

   it's been too long
   and yet i still yearn for the same thing:

   (y
      o
         u)

~ 16 ~

NEVER ENDING WALK

you wanted me to follow you
into the darkness of your own mind
but i have my own to mind

you tried to fix yourself
you didn't want me to help
thinking it would bring me hell

you were right.

it's been two months since our fall out
you would think i would be all good by now
i'm afraid not
i'm afraid i was the knot holding us together

debating whether i should call you,
i walk past your house
reminiscing over all those moments we laughed about

the silliness of my smile

crying because i'm overwhelmed by the world
i feel like i'm seven years old again
caring too intensely for people who barely even register that i am right in front of them

i feel like i'm twelve years old
my anxiety worse than it's ever been
and my depression, i'm slowly sinking in
caving to the run-down, ghostly, paranoid silhouette it wants me to be

i am nothing if not here to please.

~ 14 ~

FORMIDABLE FEELINGS

"i'm not in love"
i scoff at the accusation as my friends look at each other with knowing glances

my skin prickles
discomfort or foreboding?
discomfort at the words or the truth?
foreboding of what's about to come or cease?

or is it fear?
do i fear loving this person
or is it that i fear falling out of lo- whatever this is
because i forgot who i am without this infatuation

i'm scared of my mind
when it's not constantly thinking of you
i'm scared of the inevitable hole in my heart
that will eventually appear

it's terrifying
how one person

that you know barely
can overturn your mind
and haunt your waking days
like a phantom that will only rest when
someone else takes its place

i'm scared to let this sensation go.

~ 15 ~

STAY BACK

when the dots started to connect
and the stories aligned
it was strange for me to realise how desperately i wanted your love to be mine

i took a hearty step back
absorbing the full picture
(a fantasy i secretly longed to be true)
and realised how every one of my favourite hues spell out the name of you

my favourite artworks are influenced by your hand
i see films through the lens of your eyes
adding on the magic of being part of your life

but to you i am a mere passer-by
a slight smile in the hallways
bare acknowledgement in class

can you feel my burning gaze?

the blue of your eyes
the curved lines
of our love

god, what have you done
what have we become
maybe our love deserved that hot rod
that was speared right through us

complicated, crazy, confusing
catastrophic, calamitous
creating crying cowering hearts
haven't we done enough to screw all this up?

~ 17 ~

STOIC BOY

you think you always have to be
cool about it
so you close the doors,
open up a bottle of beer
lay back and swing a mighty sip

ignore all the emotions stirring up inside of you
ignore those who care about you –
escape, escape, escape
this place

a state of mind, they say
you believe it's physical, so off you drive down the interstate

don't feel, don't think
about it, keep a neutral face
don't even let anger show
only nonchalance, indifference

ignore everything
and

escape, escape, escape.

~ 18 ~

SHIELDED

you came from a family that seldom showed affection
unused to hugs you were, never willingly in close proximity with others
i showed you otherwise.

i introduced you to a whole new world of *love*
and as you fell in love with *love*
i fell in love with you

but just as you were unfamiliar with physical affirmations of love
your love had been meticulously stowed away
locked in a chest deep inside your heart
guarded by spiked wire and predatory animals
snarling and growling and mocking any who dare to face them

untouchable, you were
untouchable, you will remain to be to me
untouchable, your love is

but i will find a way to penetrate your scarred heart

i will find a way to be tall enough to stand on my tiptoes and stretch and strain myself
    to reach that top shelf
    to reach that jar shoved in the back
    behind the discarded memories
    behind the weapons and the wars

behind all the versions of you

~ 19 ~

IS IT?

you say the most profound sentences
i feel insignificant in your presence
that sounds bad, it isn't bad
is it?

i construct the most ardent lines about you
that's the reason they're so fervent
i feel lucky to exist at the same time as you
i feel grateful i get to be in the same vicinity as you

but you'll never recognise me
even when i humiliate myself, stumbling all over the place
spilling my guts upon the nylon floor
wishing i were someone more

prettier, funnier, god why can't i be *her*?
easily malleable i am, so i <u>will</u> like all that you like
just trust me, just give me a chance
remember my name and picture my face

so i don't have to bear this misery of being me without you

even though it's all i've ever been
regardless of even a single sign of reciprocation
i stay wondering

~ 20 ~

THREE WEEKS LATER

you say i've calmed down
but i'm only quiet now
still seething, still raging
but only at the expense of my sanity

no longer hurtling objects at you
no longer hurting the skin stretched upon my bones
starved to skinny, skipped for love
left my house to find a home

mind scattered, spouting words that don't matter
to you, but to me
they are pieces of the key
i broke all that time ago

shattered, splinted, much like the ends of my hair
pulling at my peeling scalp
the root of the cause, down at my heart
turning black and frozen forever

until i open my mouth

and it all comes out
spilling my secrets to the guy at the bar
who's only job is to make sure i pay

sinking in the weight of myself
drowning in the bottles of beer i can't stop consuming
you were the alcoholic in our relationship
why am i so desperate to replace you?

you no longer believe i've calmed down
you don't think i'm capable
i'm happy to report that you're always right

in the end

~ 21 ~

PEOPLE PLEASER

please the people so that i deserve their love
plead with the gods so that i have the personality to deserve their love
promise i'll do anything if that means deserving your love

here's my homework, just in case
here's a batch of homemade brownies, just because
here's my soul, plated up nice and pretty, just for now
here's my hair, just for free

and here
is the beginning
the start of it all

six years old - i was never tall.
i was never told
i was only laughed at
when they were being cried to

the tears aren't cute anymore
　were they ever?

you're growing up now
  wasn't i always?
you need to suck it up and stop crying
  i was trying, wasn't i?

had it ever occurred to you that maybe the tears were for something more? didn't i try to tell you of the nightmares, horrific visions, that i had?
and yet you failed to realise my curse

i bore every single sign
but i was fine !
fine with spending every moment worried that a fire would engulf the house and eat my family whole, while i watched through the flames, unable to help
i would rather die than let them die.

i was fine !
with picking at the skin on my fingers until they bled, being restless but having to push it down because i was a "good kid". i tried to avoid being disruptive, but my tears proved me to be a hindrance

i am stuck with this for eternity
that's an awful long time
i presume the fault is mine
must've failed to please someone
must've failed to plead with the gods
must've failed the only reason of my existence

after all, i am nothing if not here to please.

~ 22 ~

PROCEED WITH CAUTION

how was i to know
it would end like this
two hearts broken, the aftermath
of a bloody battle to revive what had died

did you ever hope
that we would last
did you see how fruitless the effort was
to mend what was broken?

or, like me, were you naive enough
to pray to a god you never believed in
i tried so hard to heal the wounds we received,
but you can't be the antidote when you are the poison.

~ 23 ~

SUNDAY AFTERNOON

it's a sunday afternoon
golden rays of sunlight filter through the tree leaves,
a soft breeze gently ripples across the lake
and you sit by my side, enamoured by the book you're reading.

leaning against the big oak tree
i breathe in the smells of fresh air,
sprightly leaves and vibrant flowers
a chain of daisies crown your head, making you look like the very characters you read about.

specks of light and freckles adorn your face,
and my breath is lost
by how truly sublime you are.
my own book falls from my hands
yet i make no move to retrieve it.

rendered speechless,
breathless
by the sight of you

often i'd wish you would look up from your novel every once in a while
    to laugh at my gobsmacked face
    to notice the look in my eyes
    to realise that i'll love you for more than a lifetime
    if you'll let me.

    perfectly content i am, being your friend
    but you have to see by now
    that my love really has no end

*   infinite it is,*
*   as my heart may be*
*   large and generous*
*   welcoming and deserving*
*   of your love*
*   please, just let me be*

  y   r
      u   s
   o

    the word disperses into the wind, letters scattering around the world
    i hope that you find it in time
    i hope that you love me in time

    a sunlight catcher hangs delicately above us on a tree branch,
    sending colourful shards of light over our books,

the battered blanket we sit upon, our crinkled chip bags,
and my face.

i return to reading my book,
but the words fly off the pages
i try again, determined to focus

in doing so, i fail to notice
a familiar gleam in your eyes.

~ 24 ~

FOREVERLAND

i know that somewhere out there
there's a place for us

the misfits and the queers
eccentric and eclectic
peculiar and puny

but one day
once we're out of here
we will blossom into the best versions of ourselves
far away from the jeers
closer to safety

i tell my mum of my dreams
i can just see the screams
leaking out of her body, fuming
confused, shocked, disappointed

"god, what have you done?
save my child
from this disease

please!"

she pleads to above
i work hard to stifle a scoff
look at how desperate she is
to believe me untrue
it doesn't matter, i'm gonna escape this blue
　anyway

loading the car
i say goodbye to my dad
he can't even meet my eyes
pathetic coward
i'm so glad i get to leave

as i drive out of town
i pass a familiar street
i hear your voice calling me
begging me to stay
　guilt churns in my stomach but i keep my eyes on the road ahead of me,
　gripping the wheel

***

it's been three years since i started my life
queer concerts and drag clubs every other night
sometimes my phone still rings
my mother tries talking to me
but i know she's gonna cry

"god, what have you done?
she claims she's a 'gay'
ruining her life with those fiends
help me, please!"

whatever
i'm where i belong
with the misfits and the queers
eccentric and eclectic
peculiar and pretty

keep screaming for all i care
i'm too far away to hear you

~ 25 ~

SUMMER NIGHTS LEAVE ME BLEEDING

colour seeping out of my body in the black blood that streams out of my skin
   i wake up drenched in rain

   so i get up
   shake the water drops off of me
   get changed, put shoes on
   and walk to the train station

   i get on the first train that arrives,
   not bothering to look at where it is headed
   it's empty, all the seats are available
   and yet i stand, stumbling all across the place because i am adamant on not holding on to anything
   i refuse to allow assistance

   it's an express train, i think
   because it whizzes past stations
   everything a blur
   my eyes start to hurt

the sun rises early, as it does in summer
and i reach a foreign city
as i watch the burning red glow make its debut for month

birds chirp in rejoice
flying around the sky
painting the scene with silhouettes of them

i spit on the ground,
bitter and resentful
how dare the sun be able to rise every morning
when i cannot do that on my best day

~ 26 ~

YOU CONFUSE ME TO NO END

how am i to respond to the images of dying relatives flashing through my mind?
thankfully they're all still alive in real life

what am i to do after i can't breathe for a minute or two —
just sit there, holding my tongue until i turn blue?

do you find it funny, the way i cry at your successful attempts to knock me down?
boulder after boulder, it's like you *want* to break my shoulder

then all this weight i carry
the knickknacks that burden my back
will shift to my left
and my pride will become bereft

to the princesses and pageant queens that stay ever so lean
and march they shall
maintaining the right amount of gall

oh, what am i to do
when all i am here for is to love you
but you've not a heart instead a stone
hollowed out, it's barely your own
blood that it's meant to pump out
but you've got a storeroom for that, near the valves

you don't even know how much i've worked to be here
how much i've starved, cried, almost died,
to be here.

yet you don't care, do you? not a glimmer of interest or concern flashes across your face and i know
now i know
that you were relieved to leave me that fateful june afternoon.
it may as well have been night, for the darkness that overcame my light was far too bright

a shame isn't it?
that we're over now
that we're like this now
that you don't look my way now

oh Heavenly Father
is it me you'll martyr?
or marry into stardom
oh how i wish to merely be stardust

and with a gust of wind
i extinguish,
never igniting again.

~ 27 ~

RIVERFLIES

the night yearns to be with the day
just as the moon belongs alongside the sun

fireflies buzz at the riverbank
illuminating the vegetation
igniting the adoration in our hearts

the river flows from a creek to a sea
the wind blows away the dust so we can finally see
how co-existing among the likes of you
can be most wondrous

wonder fills the sky, day and night
bubbly drinks fill my stomach
and fuzzy feelings overwhelm my heart

walking along a bridge
i ask the moon for advice
she tells me to simply look into your eyes
i sigh, knowing she is right but i cannot
fulfil what she has said

because your eyes hold the key
that has the power to unclasp my armour, my costume, my disguise
once you get close enough and i brave looking into your eyes
all my secrets will be yours to keep

for your eyes are like a potion of truth
and i succumb every time
weaker than the drink you had at my birthday party

weaker than the man who told me of your existence
weaker than the person i would've become
if i hadn't found a reason to sit at the riverbank at night and watch the fireflies
you have made me stronger and weaker simultaneously
even though i may never get it right, i am grateful for all the time
i have learnt from you

~ 28 ~

THERE IS A PATH

readily available to traverse across
in my mind

red dirt lining the path
all sorts of flies and bugs leading the way
i follow the spiders to the home of all creatures freakish

i am happy in the company of my own kind.

"but what do you mean?" they say
"you're merely just another teenage girl!"
and that is precisely it.
free me from this harrowing mortality
free me from the lies of my body
free me from the chains that drag my wrists down into the depths of the deepest, darkest ocean
i am drowning in locks of hair and mascara
i am in love with vanity
i am what you see in the mirror

a blemished face decorated with tear-streaked mascara

hair frazzled, clothes dishevelled,
skinny in some places, bulging fat in most
hair everywhere, blood everywhere
scars from your past determining your future

we will never get better
only die in this grey weather
for none of us will ever matter.

~ 29 ~

I AM SPENT

by the world
for feeling so deeply

i am cursed
with this strong sense of care
for every person i see

why can't we all be happy?
why can't we all be healthy?

why can't i just shut up every once in a while?
i am afraid of being vulnerable;
i don't want to be weak again.

i don't want someone to see my sensitivity and use it against me again.
never will i put myself in that position again.

i don't want to be scrutinised, mocked, jeered at, for my abundance of empathy my big heart should be a blessing, so stop regarding it, and me, as a curse!

2.

perhaps i was a tree in a past life
always observing, always growing
every feeling permanently lingering in the roots of my being
and even as my leaves wilt,
i still stay.

~ 30 ~

JESTER

"my god, she's sensitive!"
goodness me you're arrogant
to think that i care
about the words you spare

they hurtle my way
much like the flowers lining your grave
what a shame you escaped
only to make my existence worse than yours

oh look who it is!
the heckler that refuses to say the word heck
terrified of using the lord's name in vain
but if you're a man of the lord

do you remember that envy and greed are part of the 7 sins?
and this behaviour that you're exhibiting my way is the very pinnacle of that
so shut the hell up
and give me some luck

you were once in my place
don't think that i didn't know
of course i do
i know you better than you know yourself

keep your friends close and your enemies closer
keep on calling me sensitive
and i'll keep on calling you conceited, pretentious
imperious and contemptuous

it's a dance, it's a waltz
back and forth stepping on each other's toes
coming at each other's throats
threats and insults bouncing off of one another

i really don't care
i really don't
and you seem far more invested in this trivial battle than i ever will be
so fine, i forfeit

here's your beloved crown
go on, take your long-awaited bow
call me sensitive one more time
besides,
  you've already reached past your prime

~ 31 ~

BEAUTIFUL BOY (YOU'RE LOVELY)

you're lovely and i'd hate to see your kindness wasted
why are you spending your time by my bed?
i'm under the weather and you're under the kitchen lights
making me soup so i don't die

you're lovely and i'd hate to see your sincerity wasted
so stop giving me these thoughtful gifts
i don't understand why you seem to like me
me, a creature victim to eternal hibernation

cursed by my predecessors
blessed by this modern age
you're so lovely
i'm so hideous

purple bags and red waterlines
crazed hair and rough hands
belonging to those of a hag
oh wait! it's just the only daughter my mother ever birthed

and i don't mean to be self deprecating
only wanting to be honest
only wanting to be loved
but you're here so i guess i got what i wanted?

so why does it feel like i must always apologise
sorry for accidentally stepping on your feet as we dance
sorry for crying at the cinema
sorry for existing in the same time period as you?

oh god, you're lovely
i've never met someone so unfailingly kind
and marvellous and talented and pretty much perfect
it's kind of crazy that no one else is looking up from their phones
my own slipped out of the grip of my hands and i accidentally stood on it as i got up to make my way over to you

bury me in the locks of your hair
so rich and healthy
much like the state of your mind
(and bank account)

oh, and your smile!
so divine
simply heavenly
i have ascended to the place of greater beings

in your arms
all armour is shed, all worries are lost,
and i can breathe,

breathe in the scent of you and know that this is true

because you're lovely, and i'd hate to see your kindness wasted
so i'll accept your care towards me
because even if i may not deserve it on the basis of my being,
i know i deserve it now because i love you more than it has ever crossed your mind

i'll gladly be your waiting room
patient as ever
i'll be the vacuum that sucks up all annoying dust and dirt and debris that clutters your delicate mind
and ever-growing heart

you're so lovely that i have run out of words to articulate all there is about us
about you
and your kindness makes me tear up, too
there are just so many beautiful things about you.

~ 32 ~

MY FAVOURITE OTHERWORLDLY BEING

i'll love you more than you will ever know
so i'll sit and wait for the flowers to grow
in our linked arms
and my undying love

i'll sit under our sacred tree
trying not to see you as a deity
but that's just how i see you
a goddess, beauty that only you possess

and i am your worshipper
burning offerings at the altar
you are my religion
it's hard not to be in the same region as you

i'll love you stronger than any man ever has
i'll love you so much that you won't dare to leave
the one person that sets you free
the one person that sees all you can be

just let me be
someone who loves you so dearly
the flowers are in need of some watering
the soil is sufficient, but perhaps more sunlight could do

i just want to be *something* to you

~ 33 ~

IN BETWEEN HERE AND THERE

in between the crooked teeth that shine when you smile
in between your eyes that glint with mischief
in between the sounds of the wind and the record playing from your second-hand jukebox

in between the silence of your mothers anger
the silence of our content company
the silence of—
shhhhh

in between the wonders of the world you so deeply wish to explore
in between the wants of your dad, the words of your sister that you are desperate to prove wrong
in between the expectations placed upon you and the pressure you put upon yourself

in between our linked arms remains a gap
a parting
a barrier

in between the skin you trace
and the marks you leave
the scars i nurture

in between all the distance
of here and there
in between all the distance
of the past and present

in between
the divides of our worlds
in between
the oceans that separate us

lies a soul broken in two
looking for its partner.

~ 34 ~
I HOPE I MEET YOU AGAIN.

whether that be by fortune with a connection like my friend's cousin happens to be dating your sister in our college days that seem so far away,

or maybe it'll be by fate as we bump into each other at the record store - i'm restocking shelves and you're flicking through racks of vinyls.

i hope i meet you again
and maybe we can try being friends
even though i may love you again
i don't think i'll ever stop, in the end
forever you'll stay in my heart
and always we'll remain apart
i just hope i see your smile again.

~ 35 ~

DEAR READER

    i hope you like this poem
    i wrote it just for you

    i don't know if my words make sense
    i kind of just spew out letters and arrange them in a conventional way
    then swap the words around to make it unconventional
    i try everyday to write something really profound
    that will touch the hearts of many

    but i'm afraid
    of giving my poetry the opportunity of reception
    because if you don't understand
    then i am standing on empty land

    with nothing to hold
    nothing to own

    and if people like it?
    even more fearful i'll be

because what if eventually i won't amount to anything
all my worth will be relied on my words
but what if one day i cease to speak?

i hope you like all the poems i write
you're the only person i trust
the only person that's left

~ 36 ~

LISTEN

i love the scars on your face
they remind me of the stars in the sky
shaping wondrous constellations
(if you care to look for them)

i love the density of your hair
the volume and the way you lose hair ties and break brushes
your undefined curls seem so poetic to me
showing that beauty is always there, even if the masses remain ignorant towards it

i love the sound of your voice
the way you speak and pronounce words in your own way
funny it may be, it also provides a perspective i hadn't otherwise seen

i love the way you think
though it may not be completely coherent, i feel i can follow every train of thought,
getting lost in the webs you tangle

i love your sensitivity and empathy
possibly my most favourite thing about you
you see the world through a lens i don't possess and i learn so much from you
having a big heart isn't a curse and i want you to prove that to yourself

i just hope i can be by your side when that happens

~ 37 ~

ACKNOWLEDGEMENTS

Thank you so so so much to my wonderful friend Gemma Hay who is the artist behind the front cover!!! Isn't it spectacular? Gemma I adore you with all my heart, and thank you so much for being a part of this April Morning journey with me.

Thank you endlessly to my family. I quite literally wouldn't be here without you guys, and the fact that with your help and support I am able to *publish a book* (?!) is so mind blowing to me. I love you guys infinitely.

Thank you to my friends who have read all versions of April Morning!

Kanisha Gomes – you've been by my side for my entire writing journey, you've seen my all best and worst work. It means the world to me that you helped me with April Morning, like you have with every other writing project, and just thank you again for everything!

Isabella Fahey – possibly the coolest person I know. Thank you so much for reading April Morning (the poem) and being so supportive. I appreciate you so much.

Natalie Nagy – Thank you so so so much for your kind words and the description, April Morning couldn't have flourished without you.

Cassie Jones – Thank you SO much for taking the time to read an early copy of April Morning! I adore your poetry, and it was so fulfilling sharing mine with you.

Isabella Iu – Thanks so much!!

Evelyn Brand – You've seen most of these poems before I even dreamed of turning them into a collection, and with your support I grew to have faith in myself. Thank you so much for proof-reading April Morning.

Sena Titmarsh – my best friend. Thank you for your constant support and belief in me, I wouldn't be here without you.

Thank you to the folks at IngramSpark who made this publication possible!

And thank *you*, reader, for choosing to pick up this book and read my vulnerable writing – this is my ultimate dream, and I get to live it because of you.

About the Author

Ace Tiwari is a poet, writer, and author of both *they will always find their way back to you, regardless*, and most notably, *April Morning*. From reading all the books she got her hands on and writing since she learned how to hold a pencil, Ace has written everything — novels, poems, short stories, screenplays, and songs. Ace has won a poetry competition and has been awarded a commendation in a national contest. Between high school and writing, Ace can be found playing guitar, reading a Sally Rooney novel, or bawling her eyes out to a coming-of-age movie.